Sensible Shoes

LEADER'S GUIDE

Sharon Garlough Brown

An imprint of InterVarsity Press
Downers Grove, Illinois

InterVarsity Press
P.O. Box 1400, Downers Grove, IL 60515-1426
ivpress.com
email@ivpress.com

InterVarsity Press® is the book-publishing division of InterVarsity Christian Fellowship/USA®, a movement of students and faculty active on campus at hundreds of universities, colleges, and schools of nursing in the United States of America, and a member movement of the International Fellowship of Evangelical Students. For information about local and regional activities, visit intervarsity.org.

Scripture quotations, unless otherwise noted, are from the New Revised Standard Version Bible, copyright © 1989 National Council of the Churches of Christ in the United States of America. Used by permission. All rights reserved worldwide.

Some names and identifying information may have been changed to protect the privacy of individuals.

The publisher cannot verify the accuracy or functionality of website URLs used in this book beyond the date of publication.

Cover design and image composite: Cindy Kiple
Interior design: Daniel van Loon
Images: small girl sitting on suitcase: © susan.k./Getty Images
          meadow/prairie: © Xuanyu Han / Moment Collection / Getty Images

ISBN 978-0-8308-2874-6 (print)
ISBN 978-1-5140-0363-3 (digital)

Printed in the United States of America ♾

InterVarsity Press is committed to ecological stewardship and to the conservation of natural resources in all our operations. This book was printed using sustainably sourced paper.

Library of Congress Cataloging-in-Publication Data

A catalog record for this book is available from the Library of Congress.

P	25	24	23	22	21	20	19	18	17	16	15	14	13	12	11	10	9	8	7	6	5	4	3	2	1
Y	41	40	39	38	37	36	35	34	33	32	31	30	29	28	27	26	25	24	23	22	21

CONTENTS

WELCOME

⚭

Sensible Shoes is an unusual novel, blending a fictional story with nonfiction teaching elements. Some readers view it only as a story of four characters on a journey. Others say yes to a deeper level of reading, embracing the opportunity to take a "sacred journey" along with the characters, by opening themselves to the Spirit's work and attending to God's invitations. Though many book clubs read and discuss *Sensible Shoes* based on themes, characters, and plot, the material in this guide is designed to move participants into self-reflection and prayer.

THE STORY BEHIND THE STORY

In September of 2008 I began leading a weekly women's spiritual formation group at the church where my husband, Jack, and I copastored. I had led many kinds of groups over the years—Bible studies, prayer groups, pastoral care groups, and book discussions—and I thought I knew what this Monday morning group of twelve women would become. I planned to lead a study on spiritual disciplines, using one of the many excellent resources about ways we can cooperate with the Holy Spirit's work of conforming us to Jesus Christ.

By our second meeting, however, I was convinced that the Lord was asking me to drop the idea of a book study. Instead, he was inviting me to trust him by journeying without a syllabus or curriculum. So I began to introduce the group to spiritual disciplines that had impacted my life with God, such as prayerfully reading the Word (lectio divina), the prayer of examen, journaling, labyrinth prayer, praying with imagination, and spiritual direction. Our time together became sacred space where we encountered the living God. As we practiced sitting in stillness and silence, we became more attentive listeners, not only to God but to one another.

In one of our first meetings together, one of the women in the group looked around the circle and commented, "Everybody here is wearing really cute, but sensible shoes!" The phrase stuck, and we started referring to ourselves as the

"Sensible Shoes Club." God was leading us through the unpredictable and often treacherous terrain of the inner life, and we needed sensible shoes for the journey. We also needed one another.

Over the next couple of months, we witnessed stunning and breathtakingly beautiful transformation as the Lord opened blind eyes, revealed old wounds, and set captives free. In November of 2008 I sensed that God was calling me to write about the role of spiritual disciplines in our formation in Christ, both individually and in community. Since there were already so many good nonfiction resources available, I felt led toward writing it as a fictional story. What would happen, I wondered, if I created four characters who met at a retreat center in order to learn ways to walk more closely with God?

As I prayed about that idea, Meg, Hannah, Mara, and Charissa began to emerge from my imagination, each of them wrestling with common issues: letting go of control, perfectionism, shame, regret, fear, people pleasing, and hiding behind roles and busyness. Each of them is invited to travel deeper into the heart of God and to discover the height and depth, length and breadth of his love. They're invited to know God and know themselves more intimately. And they're invited to say yes to the gift of community. Though none of the characters was based directly on people from my group, the heart of their journey toward freedom was the heart of our journey as well.

THE SHAPE OF THIS GUIDE

Part one of this book provides resources and background for a twelve-week small group experience through *Sensible Shoes* using the *Sensible Shoes Study Guide*, an in-depth supplementary resource for spiritual formation.

Part two offers content and schedules for various kinds of retreat experiences with *Sensible Shoes*—whether one-day, weekend, or online.

A third approach would be to combine the two options to include both an opening or closing retreat and ongoing small group sessions. For example, you could conclude your twelve-week small group with a *Sensible Shoes* Retreat to practice the disciplines in a more extended way together. You could invite others to join you on retreat and then launch a new twelve-week small group out of that experience.

When I finished writing *Sensible Shoes* in 2009, I had two primary prayers: first, that the Lord would use the book to facilitate an encounter with him and bring healing and transformation to readers, and second, that the book would provide an invitation to readers to travel deeper into the love of God in community.

Your saying yes to leading a group or facilitating a retreat is an answer to my prayers. Thank you for paying attention to God's nudge forward. I hope this guide will provide helpful tips and insights as you lead.

PART ONE

Leading Small Groups

INTRODUCTION

Experiencing Transformation

∞

I'm often asked whether the degree of transformation the characters experience in *Sensible Shoes* is "realistic." Based on what I witnessed in the first Sensible Shoes Club, yes—even in a relatively short amount of time. But our group began with an important gift: every single person who committed to the group had a common longing for creating and guarding a safe space where we could be unmasked and unafraid with one another and with God. Our souls are timid creatures, and we will not come out from hiding and name what is true if we think we will be rejected, judged, condemned, or gossiped about.

As the leader of the group, it was important for me to model authenticity and vulnerability as much as possible so that others felt free to share as well. It was also important to keep reminding the group of our commitment to be trustworthy stewards of one another's stories. In essence, what we said to each other was this: "By the grace of God I will be for you what I long for you to be for me."

As a leader you're invited to consider your own spiritual formation, not just as you read and reflect on the material in the book, but also as you lead others in reflection and conversation. Each week you'll be provided with a few prayer prompts for your work as a leader, tips for facilitating the group, and behind-the-scenes information about the characters and their journeys. Feel free to share these "bonus features" about the characters or my writing process, perhaps as an opening or icebreaker. Since the purpose of your meeting is for spiritual formation and prayer, however, watch for how group members may be tempted to divert conversation into a book club discussion rather than an exploration of how the characters are serving as windows and mirrors to see God and yourselves more clearly.

Because of our group's commitment to transparency, we grew to trust one another deeply. Not only were we able to receive comfort as we honestly named struggles, losses, and grief, but we were also able to receive the assurance of God's love and grace as we confessed sin, shame, failures, and regret to one another. James speaks the truth when he tells us to confess our sins to one another and pray for each other so that we can be healed (James 5:16). Our group met together nearly every week for five years. To this day, I speak with deep gratitude and awe about what the Lord did in us, for us, and through us.

I pray God's blessing upon you as you say yes to the journey in community. May the Lord reveal himself to you in life-giving, transformational ways. May he fill you with grace, give you courage, and empower you with his Spirit. And may you experience profound healing and joy as you keep company with him, together.

Frequently Asked Questions

How many people should be in the group? Ideally, no fewer than four and no more than twelve. My original Sensible Shoes Club had twelve, and it worked for us. But we met for two and a half hours every week, which gave plenty of time for prayer and conversation. Larger groups might wish to gather together at the beginning of a session, then subdivide into smaller groups, each with a designated facilitator, for conversation and prayer. If you subdivide into small groups, remain with the same group for the whole study.

Do I need to be a trained spiritual director or ministry leader to facilitate a group? No. Though it might help if you've already had experience leading a group, the best gift you bring is your own pursuit of God and your openness to the Lord shaping and forming you, not only in the past but also as you participate in the study.

Is it important for people to already know each other well when the group starts? No. Even groups that have been together a long time might find that this study leads them into unfamiliar, even uncomfortable territory of deep reflection and conversation. If you don't have an established group, don't be afraid of inviting people who wouldn't normally choose to connect with one another. Diversity of age, experience, and background can be a rich gift.

Do we need to meet weekly? Though the twelve-week study is designed for weekly group interaction, some groups meet every other week. However, since there is so much content to process, I don't recommend combining multiple weeks into a single session. You'll be best served by taking the journey as slowly as you need to, even if that means a longer time commitment.

Do we need to have one designated leader for the group, or can we rotate facilitation? Do whatever best serves the desires, dynamics, and gifts of your group. If there is one designated leader for the entire study, that leader can discern whether to participate fully in the discussion by sharing personal insights, or whether their role is primarily to moderate discussion and encourage others to share their experiences.

Should we allow new people to join our group after we begin? Approach this prayerfully, as each group will be different. While adding a group member for the second session likely won't create much upheaval, I recommend having an honest conversation during your first session to see whether members are open to this. If you add new group members, have one-on-one conversations before their first meeting to summarize your opening session and talk about their hopes and expectations for the study. It's difficult (though not impossible) to add new people after several sessions, not only because the trust level has been established in the group but because groups inevitably begin to shorthand their experience together, potentially causing a newcomer to feel disoriented or excluded.

Before You Begin

Each participant will need a copy of *Sensible Shoes: A Story About the Spiritual Journey* and the *Sensible Shoes Study Guide*. Participants can decide whether they prefer to read the whole book first or read only the designated chapters each week. (Many people discover that the second reading of the book yields invitations they didn't notice the first time around.)

Set up your meeting space so that everyone is on the same level and seated in a circle if possible, as a table between you creates a barrier. Try to eliminate distractions in the environment, and ask everyone to silence and put away any devices.

Before group members begin the week one study, send a welcome email to highlight these elements from the *Study Guide* introduction:

* Please bring a Bible, pen, and notebook to each session. The *Sensible Shoes Journal*, a lightly-lined notebook, which includes quotes from the book, serves as a good travelogue for the journey.

* Don't worry if you don't have time or capacity to answer each question every day. Answer the ones you're able to answer. Even if you don't feel prepared for the group session, come anyway. (You will likely need to repeat this reassurance and invitation many times throughout the study.)

* To frame each day with the Word, first read the Scripture text (marked in bold in the exercises). Then journal your responses to the questions.

LEADER'S NOTES ON EACH SESSION

....

Week One

BEHIND-THE-SCENES VIEW

When I started writing my manuscript in 2008, I knew there would be four characters who would meet at a retreat center, but I knew nothing else about them. So I asked the Lord to help me see one thing that had happened to each woman when she was a little girl so I could understand where she was stuck or struggling as an adult. As I prayed, images and scenes emerged: Meg hunting for the bells, Hannah concealing her sorrow over her "fixed" teddy bear, Mara being picked last for a team, and Charissa not getting the highest score on a math test. (Charissa's flashback would eventually be moved to a later chapter in the book.)

The cover of *Sensible Shoes* reflects the importance of childhood experiences in shaping and forming us. I gaze at the top photo and wonder, *Who is the little girl sitting on the suitcase? Where has she come from and where is she going? And is anyone traveling with her?*

As a contrast to the solitary journey of the child, the bottom photo represents the invitation to community and depicts hope as we travel together. None of the characters is physically portrayed by the women in the photo. (Readers are often confused about this and try to figure out who's who.) But note how the woman on the far left lags a few steps behind, while the woman to her right extends her hand to urge her forward. Those women could be any of the characters at any stage of their journey. They could be us as well. Along the journey we will experience reluctance and hope—sometimes simultaneously!

EXPLORING THE LEADERSHIP LANDSCAPE

Because of her professional training and ministry experience, Hannah is likely to become the default leader of the group of four. She is also the one most likely to hide. Her role of leadership is protective for her, part of a well-constructed defense mechanism that keeps her from revealing her own heart. Though Hannah is never one to dominate conversation in a group, she is skilled at offering just enough personal information to make others feel as if they've connected with her. She often deflects attention away from herself by inviting others to come out from hiding to reveal intimate details about their own lives. She has finely honed skills of manipulation.

* Do you identify with Hannah in any of these ways? If so, these aren't issues to be resolved before you begin your leadership (or an opportunity for self-condemnation). Just be aware of any similar inner dynamics. If you don't already have a spiritual director, mentor, or trustworthy friend, ask God to lead you toward someone who can provide confidential support for you as you lead.

* Prayerfully discern what your role is in the group. Are you a co-participant, freely sharing insights from your own prayerful engagement with the content? Or are you primarily a moderator, helping to keep the group on track, gently redirecting conversation when necessary, and encouraging members to participate? Or perhaps somewhere in the middle? Your role may evolve during the study as the group becomes more comfortable and grows in trust. But you might want to share honestly at the beginning what you expect your role to be.

* Regardless of how deeply you will share from your own personal experience, remember that God invites you to a sacred journey as well. As you write your RSVP for the journey, focus on God's call to you as a leader. How are you feeling about his call? What are your hopes, fears, longings, or hesitations? Speak honestly with God about these things.

NAVIGATIONAL TIPS

* As part of your welcome to the group, read the "Note from Sharon" on page 10 of the *Study Guide*. Return to this note frequently as a reminder, since this way of being together may be different than what people have experienced before. You might also mention that we don't have to use words

to communicate judgment, rejection, and condemnation. Remember: Charissa speaks fluent eyebrow and can quickly shame someone with facial expressions and body language.

* If your group hasn't been together before, you might want to do an additional icebreaker after you ask each person to share a hope for the study (*Study Guide*, p. 10). Gather some props that represent the characters in chapter one: bell (Meg), pruning shears (Hannah), book (Charissa), baseball glove or other sports item (Mara). Have a brief conversation about what each of the items reveals about who the women are. This can provide a good segue into the Scripture reading and questions about the characters.

* Let the characters do the heavy lifting for getting conversations started, especially in your first few sessions. When we can see the issues they're struggling with, we might more easily move into self-disclosure and discover solidarity. It's a gift when we hear someone else's story and realize, "You too? I thought I was the only one!"

....

Week Two

BEHIND-THE-SCENES VIEW

While none of the characters are based on real people, each of them received different parts of me. Meg received my sensitivity and some of my fears. Hannah received my overdeveloped sense of responsibility and the compulsion to define myself by my productivity and usefulness. Charissa received my perfectionism and some of my socially acceptable idols, including the pursuit of honor, esteem, and high achievement. And Mara received my childhood wound of always being the last one picked for an athletic team.

I often hear from readers who say, "I saw myself in each of the characters but especially in [fill in the blank.]" Throughout the study, remind your group members that seeing ourselves more clearly is meant to be a gift of grace in our lives, not a source of embarrassment or shame. We are all in process, and

God regards us with far more tenderness and compassion than we often extend to ourselves.

EXPLORING THE LEADERSHIP LANDSCAPE

Katherine cautions the "pilgrims" that the journey toward freedom and transformation isn't easy and requires courage (*Sensible Shoes*, p. 51). Even in the first two weeks of questions and reflections, members of your group may be feeling a sense of disequilibrium or discouragement. Like Meg, some might feel the group is "too advanced" for them, and they're ready to escape through the nearest exit door. Or, like Charissa, some may be suspicious of the content of the study, and they communicate their skepticism through subtle or overt ways that are potentially disruptive to community. Not only are the members likely to experience personal upheaval from the Spirit, but the discomfort and mess they encounter in their own lives will inevitably affect group life. Some, like Mara, will share intimate details of their insights and struggles, while others will be uncomfortable with that level of disclosure. Holding sacred space for a group in formation is a challenge.

* Take Katherine's words to heart, not only in your personal journey but as the leader God has chosen and called: "Don't be afraid of the mess. The Holy Spirit is a faithful guide, gently shepherding and empowering [you] as [you] travel more deeply into the heart of God" (p. 51). What do you need from God as you shepherd others in the journey? Speak honestly with him about whatever comes to mind.

* Are there any group members who are already testing your patience? Why might they be pushing your buttons? Speak with God about this. And ask for the grace to pray for them.

* If, like Hannah, you find yourself too preoccupied with others' journeys to attend to your own, what are God's invitations to you?

NAVIGATIONAL TIPS

For walking the labyrinth.

* If you're walking a labyrinth as a group, it may help to spend the first few minutes reviewing the handout together (*Sensible Shoes*, p. 55). Reassure the group that there's no right or wrong way to pray while you

walk. Depending on your group size (and the size of the labyrinth), you may need to stagger entries onto the path.

* It's a different experience walking the labyrinth in solitude versus walking it in community, and both can be fruitful times of prayer. Encourage your group members to be open and receptive to whatever surfaces as they walk and pray—without judging it or comparing it to what others seem to be experiencing. Our discomfort and resistance can also be revealing.

* Give space for debriefing, asking general questions such as, "What was that experience like for you?" and specific questions such as, "What did you notice as you walked and prayed?"

For group discussion.

* Because *Sensible Shoes* is written with an intimate point of view, readers have access to unedited interior monologues. This week you get to hear the characters' thoughts as they meet one another for the first time: the ways they silently compare and measure themselves against each other, judge themselves, and prejudge others. As an entry point into discussion this week, you might want to name our inevitable temptation to do the same. Don't be afraid to laugh at yourselves if you find your own insecurities or critical spirits voiced by the characters. Identifying the "elephant in the room" can be an opportunity to deepen solidarity and authenticity with one another.

* Throughout your journey together, you're likely to encounter resistance about various disciplines. Sadly, the labyrinth can be particularly divisive. Though archaeologists have discovered labyrinths in Christian churches dating as far back as the fourth century, we have no historical record of how these were used in worship. It's possible that during the Middle Ages Christians used cathedral labyrinths to simulate pilgrimage to Jerusalem, but this is speculation.

* If there's fear or resistance in your group regarding labyrinths, watch for any impulse to become defensive. Instead, go gently with one another and use my note (*Study Guide*, p. 20) as a reminder about Christian freedom and the priority of being rooted in mutual love.

Week Three

BEHIND-THE-SCENES VIEW

As I wrote the first draft of *Sensible Shoes*, I knew it was important to let the story unfold in a way that was true for each character, without trying to control their journeys. That meant I didn't outline or plan any details in advance. Instead, the characters had freedom to walk on and off the page, even if that complicated the story.

When the women returned for their second of six retreat sessions, Meg chose her previous seat at the back of the room, near the exit. But Charissa, who hadn't meaningfully connected with anyone during the first session, sat at the front. I knew immediately that this was "true" for her: by temperament, she's a front-row learner who had ended up at the back table during the first session only because Katherine had asked some participants to move to tables that didn't have enough people. As soon as Hannah entered the room, I knew she would sit by Meg, just in case Meg needed pastoral care. And when Meg asked Hannah if she had seen Mara, and Hannah shook her head, I thought to myself, *I haven't seen her either. And I don't know if she's coming.*

At that point, the whole story threatened to unravel. What would happen if my four characters stopped sitting together—or if one of them disappeared completely? What if community didn't develop? Wasn't that the whole point of the book?

EXPLORING THE LEADERSHIP LANDSCAPE

There may be points along the journey when your group threatens to unravel too. Not everyone is prepared for the rigors of deep reflection, especially in a group setting. That's okay. Be willing to let someone depart from the group with your blessing. It's also possible that someone in the group will decide this is not the study they wanted or expected. See if they are open to a conversation about exploring the reasons why. If, like Meg or Mara, they feel as if they aren't "good enough," use the characters' fears and insecurities to encourage them to see that they do belong and are welcome.

✳ Pay attention to any impulse to try to control or manage someone else's journey. How comfortable are you with giving people freedom to make their own choices, even if you don't agree with them? Speak with God about what you notice.

✳ Are you apt to become defensive or irritable when someone rejects what you offer? What does this response reveal about what you need from God?

✳ Prayerfully watch for those who might need a word of encouragement to help them stay engaged. Is there anyone in the group who might benefit from a personal email or phone call or face-to-face conversation?

Navigational Tips

✳ This week you've been exploring some potentially tender places by identifying early and current images of God. If people are reluctant to share their own images, focus first on what the characters see. Note how their images were formed and what God's invitations are to them now.

✳ For Mara, her image of God as El Roi, the God who sees, began as a word of grace but deteriorated into a word of judgment and needs to be restored or replaced by something new. For Charissa, her image of God as Helper is a biblical image but has been a self-centered one (the God who has helped her succeed), and she doesn't yet see this. For Meg, her image of God as Shepherd is a childhood image that she is invited to understand more deeply as an adult. For Hannah, her image of God as the Father who fixes things has died, and she's not sure what has risen in its place. She only sees her own visceral reaction against the image of God as Lover, and she is reluctant to explore her strong reaction.

✳ In examining our images of God, it's important to discern whether they are biblical images, deeply rooted in the revelation of God in Scripture and in the person and work of Jesus Christ. If someone offers an image of God that isn't biblical, watch prayerfully for how God would lead you to respond. What questions might you ask that help someone move toward healing and freedom? It's not your job (or anyone else's in the group) to "fix it," but rather to point gently to truth and encourage further reflection.

* You may wish to invite everyone to name their images aloud, just like the group did at New Hope (*Sensible Shoes*, p. 100). You can speak them as part of a group prayer or write them down as a record of how you currently know and name God. Keep encouraging the group to be attentive both to images that attract and images that repel.

....

Week Four

BEHIND-THE-SCENES VIEW

After I introduced our Sensible Shoes Club to several different spiritual practices, our group settled into the weekly practice of corporate lectio divina. Four different women would read the short Scripture text, each reading followed by silence. After the fourth reading we would continue in silence, journaling about whatever we had noticed in our time of prayer. Then we would share those insights with one another. We were always amazed at how uniquely the Holy Spirit spoke to us through the Word.

For the first few months of our practice, I chose Scripture texts I thought would be fruitful for us to meditate on. Then I sensed the Lord asking me to give up that control, so group members began offering suggestions. Eventually, we decided to use the Revised Common Lectionary. When we gathered on a Monday morning, we would look at the five suggested texts for the week and select one for meditation. Since our congregation used the lectionary to shape our worship services (readings, prayers, and sermon), it was a wonderful way for us to dwell deeply in the Word as preparation for our corporate worship.

Though I chose John 1:35-39 as the text Katherine would use with the group, I did not try to control how Charissa responded to it. Instead, I prayerfully listened to the text as if I were Charissa, watching for what might catch her attention. Her suspicion, resentment, and irritability over "losing control" of the text emerged in the process of prayer, and the Word continued to pursue her in ways that provoked her toward deeper reflection.

EXPLORING THE LEADERSHIP LANDSCAPE

Katherine advises the group not to worry about practicing lectio divina "correctly," saying, "If you attempt to turn this into a method to master, you will have missed the point" (*Sensible Shoes*, p. 104). As you prepare for your meeting, be aware of any anxiety that might arise in you about "doing things right" as you lead the exercise. If you are new to this way of meditating on Scripture, be honest with your group. You can all be learners together.

* Consider your own relationship to God's Word. Have you read Scripture as a task? Obligation? In order to use it to teach others? Have you read God's Word primarily for information or for transformation? Talk with God about what you notice. What longings stir within you?

* As a personal prayer exercise this week, read John 1:35-39 from the perspective of John the Baptist. What is it like to point others to Jesus? How do you feel when they detach from you and attach to Jesus? What is your prayer for them as they go? What is your prayer for yourself?

NAVIGATIONAL TIPS

* Even though you and your group have already prayed with John 1:35-39 this week, meditating on the same text together not only introduces people to the richness of the corporate practice of this discipline but also provides an opportunity to practice hearing the text in a fresh way. Invite group members to lay aside what they've already heard in the text and be open to receiving something new.

* Before you begin, you may want to emphasize that this is a different discipline than studying God's Word. Lectio divina is an ancient way of praying with Scripture and may be unfamiliar or uncomfortable (as it is for Charissa). Some in your group may share reflections that sound more like Bible study responses. That's okay. A gentle follow-up question may open them to consider how the Spirit is bringing the Word to life for them in an intimate way.

* There may be some in your group who "don't hear anything" when they pray with the text. Reassure them that this is okay too. If their thoughts drift

to measuring and comparing themselves against others (e.g., "Other people always have profound insights, and I never have any"), suggest that feeling "less than" could be the starting point for their conversation with God today.

* Consider carrying forward the practice of lighting a Christ candle every time you gather.

....

Week Five

BEHIND-THE-SCENES VIEW

When I wrote *Sensible Shoes* in 2008–2009, I had been a pastor for many years. But I had only just begun training as a spiritual director. Because I didn't feel as if I could authentically inhabit the interior life of a seasoned spiritual director, readers are never in Katherine's point of view while she's offering direction. (By the time I wrote *Two Steps Forward*, I had completed my training and was serving as a spiritual director, so Katherine becomes a point-of-view character.)

Though I prayed throughout the writing of the book, I was particularly attentive for God's guidance whenever I wrote any of Katherine's words. I knew readers would give her wisdom weight, and it was important that what she offered be rooted in her own prayerful listening.

Sometimes Katherine's words surprised me, and I would close my computer, throw my hands up, and whisper my thanks for the gift. Sometimes I gave Katherine images or insights I had received from the Lord in my own life. And sometimes Katherine speaks with gracious words I've received from others. The words she offers Meg about fears becoming opportunities for intimacy with God (pp. 148-49) were some of the last I wrote for *Sensible Shoes* and emerged out of my own journey from fear to love.

EXPLORING THE LEADERSHIP LANDSCAPE

When Charissa decides to talk with Dr. Allen about the sacred journey retreat, we don't have access to his thoughts. Because we're in Charissa's point of view, we can only see and hear what she sees and hears, filtered through her thoughts and feelings. Though she attempts to wear a mask with him, we know how confused, offended, and angry she is. At the end of chapter five, however, we enter Nathan Allen's point of view for the first time. We now have access to his thoughts, feelings, and discernment process. We learn he's second-guessing how much truth he spoke. He's wondering if he pushed her too hard. And we learn about a painful memory this experience has tapped in him.

* Reflect on your leadership journey so far. Do you share anything in common with Nathan or the way he's processing what happened with Charissa? Speak with God about anything you notice.

* Nathan remembers Katherine's wisdom about two people potentially hearing the same words in vastly different ways (*Sensible Shoes*, p. 140). Have you seen evidence of this in your group? How is God helping you navigate leadership challenges?

* Nathan has deep compassion for Charissa because he sees in her many of the same weaknesses and sins that he has seen in himself. Often, though, we become most frustrated with people who mirror our own weaknesses and sins. Is there anyone in the group who is frustrating you right now? Why? How might God enlarge your compassion? Spend some time praying for any members you find challenging.

NAVIGATIONAL TIPS

* As the journey continues, characters may become increasingly frustrating to your group members, and people are likely to disagree about who is frustrating and why. If group members aren't yet taking to heart the saying, "Learn to linger with what provokes you," remind them that frustration can be a gift indicating where the Spirit is longing to heal us and set us free.

* If the characters and their journeys begin to dominate your conversation (as they would in a book club), keep drawing the group's attention back to personal insights about opportunities for spiritual formation and growth.

❋ As necessary, remind the group of the promises you made to one another at the beginning of the journey and the invitation not to "fix" or offer advice (*Study Guide*, p. 10). Is your group becoming more comfortable with shared silence? If not, how might you highlight this as a corporate practice?

....

Week Six

BEHIND-THE-SCENES VIEW

Throughout the writing process, the characters surprised, delighted, and sometimes frustrated me. As I got to know them, I discovered they had experienced sorrows that broke my heart. They made decisions I didn't agree with. And they moved toward God in ways that made me rejoice. I often say that they feel more "revealed" than "created."

I'll never forget the moment I realized that two of my characters shared a past. Nathan was on his sailboat, wondering whether he had pushed Charissa too hard. Then his thoughts shifted to someone he knew in graduate school. The more he revealed about her, the more my heart started to race. I stopped typing and exclaimed, "Wait! Do you know Hannah Shepley?" Running upstairs, I called out to Jack, "You're never gonna believe this! Hannah and Dr. Allen actually know each other!" Though Nathan's reappearance complicates Hannah's plans for her sabbatical, it will eventually serve as the impetus for her to examine some of her wounds.

EXPLORING THE LEADERSHIP LANDSCAPE

Hannah continues to focus on others as an avoidance strategy. Though she can perceive how other people have lived in denial, she has blind spots about her own grief.

❋ Scan your journey as a leader over the past six weeks. Have you been able to attend to your own spiritual formation journey while encouraging others? Do you notice any distraction or avoidance strategies in yourself? Speak with God about whatever you see.

* How are you currently navigating the balance between personal disclosure and facilitating group conversation? Is anything evolving in your leadership style as you move forward together? What are God's invitations to you, both personally and in your role as a leader?

NAVIGATIONAL TIPS

* Katherine mentions that the prayer of examen has been one of her most important daily disciplines. (This has been true for me too.) It's not a long process—just ten to fifteen minutes of prayerful review, typically practiced at the end of the day (or at noon and end of day). Emphasize the study guide's direction to practice it as many days as possible, while reminding the group that as with the characters, we will likely struggle to form new habits of prayer. No condemnation!

* The palms-up, palms-down prayer (which I learned from author Richard Foster) is a simple way of centering ourselves in the presence of God. It's a prayer practice you could easily incorporate into future sessions, perhaps after you light your Christ candle.

Week Seven

BEHIND-THE-SCENES VIEW

When I realized that Hannah had continued a daily practice of lectio divina in the Gospel of John, I mentally calculated how far she might have read since their group session with John 1:35-39, and I ended up with the wedding at Cana. I had no idea how that text would break her open. Hannah's lament on the beach is a watershed moment for her as she comes out from behind her mask and tells God the truth about her disappointment, anger, and sorrow.

After Hannah collapsed on the beach, I spent several days writing scenes that went nowhere. Every time I tried to send Meg to the cottage to help her, I felt blocked. "I have no idea how she's going to move forward," I said to Jack one day. "She's in a really hard place."

He replied, "If she were real, you would trust God to reach her, wouldn't you?"

Yes. I would. That's when I saw how I was trying to interfere and make things easier for her instead of letting her sit with her sorrow. I needed to back away from my attempts to control her healing and wait for God to work.

EXPLORING THE LEADERSHIP LANDSCAPE

The impulse to rescue and mitigate suffering for my character was the same impulse the Lord had confronted in me years earlier as a pastor. There were times when my rushing into a situation circumvented the Spirit's deeper, slower work. Picture watching a butterfly struggling to emerge from a cocoon. We might think the compassionate response is to intervene. But the struggle to emerge from the binding strengthens the wings. Rather than trying to help, sometimes we're called to wait, watch, and pray.

* What has compassionate care looked like in your life? In your group?

* When have you been tempted to rush, help, or fix rather than wait, watch, and pray? Speak with God about whatever you notice.

NAVIGATIONAL TIPS

* Though we might not be surprised by Charissa's harsh (silent) judgment and rejection of Mara at the beach picnic, Hannah shows an ugly manipulative side that sets Mara up for rejection. This scene may surface strong emotions in group members who have been shamed or emotionally abused, and those who identify with Mara and her past may need some extra attention and compassionate care.

* When teaching about the examen, Katherine says that some people (like Meg) will find it easier to review times when they were brought to life and experienced God's presence and harder to confront the hiddenness of God or their darker feelings (*Sensible Shoes*, p. 194). Others (like Mara) will find it more natural to focus on sorrow and loss and harder to see blessings and gifts (p. 198). You might wish to survey the group to see how they self-identify in this regard. Keep in mind that depending on which way they personally lean, some group members

will also find it harder to hear others express either consolation or desolation. How might you encourage the naming of both, privately and corporately, without privileging one over the other?

✳ If members are willing to share their laments, frame this as a corporate prayer time, taking turns to read your prayers. Give a time of silence after reading each lament so that all can join in offering it to God.

....

Week Eight

BEHIND-THE-SCENES VIEW

Just before *Sensible Shoes* was published, I talked with my spiritual director about the process of releasing my book into the world. "I hear some fear in you," she commented. "Do you know what that's about?"

I had already prayed through some of the more obvious fears about rejection and criticism. But this fear was deeper. "I'm afraid that the book might stir up strong emotions and tap some tender wounds in readers," I said. "And I'm really worried that some of them might not have community alongside as they process their pain. I'm worried they'll be overwhelmed." I told her there was a particular page in the book where Katherine pleads with the characters not to walk alone (p. 229). "I wish I could put her words in bold print with an asterisk on the bottom of the page saying, Please listen!"

She looked at me and said gently, "Sharon, can you trust the Spirit to bring into bold print anything a reader might need in her life with God?"

Her words of wisdom penetrated me. I had trusted God to inspire me as I wrote the book. Could I now trust God to shepherd the ones who read it? Could I surrender my desire for control and let go of my overdeveloped sense of responsibility? Could I commit readers into God's safekeeping and care, no matter how they might react to my work?

EXPLORING THE LEADERSHIP LANDSCAPE

Before she leads their fourth session, Katherine kneels in the chapel to pray for the group (p. 223). She knows that some of them are feeling overwhelmed and discouraged, so she wraps her prayer around God's word of comfort through the prophet Isaiah.

* How is God inviting you to pray for your group right now? For yourself?

* Are there any burdens God is calling you to lay down as you move forward in leadership? How is God longing to care for you as you care for others?

Navigational Tips

* Take the group's temperature regarding fatigue (emotional, spiritual, mental, physical). Ask each person to share a few words or an image that describes how they're feeling about the journey right now. After each person shares, hold silence for a moment of prayer. Then move into lectio divina with Psalm 121.

* For some in your group, George Herbert's poem may feel too remote or intellectual. That's okay! Remind them that God meets us where we are, uniquely tailoring images or experiences that will catch our attention and resonate with us. That's part of his intimacy with us.

....

Week Nine

Behind-the-Scenes View

My first spiritual director, a Dominican sister, still laughs about the first time she invited me to pray with my imagination. "I'm sorry," I said. "I don't do that. I'm a Protestant."

When Katherine speaks to the group about her initial hesitation over praying with imagination, she speaks from my own experience of reluctance. Like Charissa, I have a rather rigorous "orthodoxy detector." Because I was well-trained in biblical study and exegesis, this spiritual discipline landed in my suspect box.

Ironically, the text Sister Diane had invited me to enter imaginatively was the encounter between Nicodemus and Jesus. God has a sense of humor. Years later, I could tell you many stories of how the Spirit has blown as I've prayed this way. I'm continually amazed by what the Lord brings to the surface when I say yes to yielding control over what a text "means" and relax into a more playfully curious posture with him.

It was an utter delight to watch the wind blow freely as Meg, Charissa, and Mara prayed with the Bartimaeus story, each of them uniquely encountering Jesus as they pictured themselves in the scene. I was as surprised as they were by what emerged!

Exploring the Leadership Landscape

Throughout the study you may have encountered resistance to various spiritual practices, in yourself and in the group.

* How have you navigated resistance personally? In your leadership?

* How has God used resistance to catch your attention and invite you into deeper life, both individually and in community?

Navigational Tips

* If possible, place a bouquet of flowers in the center of your circle as a reminder of God's love.

* Depending on your group dynamics, it may be helpful to prime the pump for praying with imagination together by talking briefly about each character's experience of resonance and resistance with the exercise.

* Some in the group will thrive with this practice. Others will struggle. Encourage people to be honest about the obstacles they face when praying this way.

* Charissa's courage in confessing her sin to Mara opens the opportunity for Mara to extend generosity and grace and paves the way for an unlikely friendship. How might their example speak to your life together?

Week Ten

BEHIND-THE-SCENES VIEW

Katherine invites Meg to ponder the meaning of her name ("pearl") and how it connects with her life. But Meg isn't the only one whose name is symbolic.

Meg Fowler Crane: When the book opens Meg is flitting like a little bird around the yard, searching for bells. Fowler, her maiden name, means, "one who hunts or traps birds." Meg is ensnared by fears and grief, even as she admires her sister and daughter for their wings. While some cranes migrate long distances, other cranes don't migrate at all. Meg's marriage to Jim Crane was a brief period when she experienced the joy and freedom of flight.

Hannah Shepley: Hannah ("grace") is named for the heartbroken, barren woman who begs God for a child in 1 Samuel. Hannah is given a nine-month sabbatical (pregnancy image) and feels the weight of her barrenness, even as God is forming something new in her. Shepley means "from the sheep meadow" and seemed an appropriate name for one who was reluctant to leave her flock.

Mara Payne Garrison: Mara ("bitter") is named for the waters that are too bitter for the Hebrews to drink during their wandering in the wilderness. It is also the name Naomi says she should be called after she suffers severe losses (Ruth 1:20). Mara's childhood was full of pain (Payne), and her marriage is like a fortress where she first thought she would be protected and defended (Garrison), but now she feels trapped.

Charissa Goodman Sinclair: Charissa knows her name means "grace." (*Charis* is the Greek word for "grace.") But she thinks of grace in terms of elegance and refinement. Her journey will lead her toward being converted out of her works righteousness (Goodman) into God's grace. Sinclair means "clear sight." Charissa is invited to "come and see," and she begins to understand how blind she has been.

Katherine Rhodes: Katherine ("pure") is a trustworthy leader for a group that is exploring ways ("roads") to travel deeper into the heart of God.

EXPLORING THE LEADERSHIP LANDSCAPE

Each of the characters has images or metaphors that describe where they have been. They also have images or metaphors that speak to where they are going.

* What images or metaphors have emerged in your own life the past couple of months?

* What images or metaphors have emerged in your life as a group?

* How do these images or metaphors give you hope and encourage you as you move forward, individually and corporately?

NAVIGATIONAL TIPS

* Each of the characters is experiencing deep sorrow right now. Often when we're grieving, we hear the message, "Get over it." We might even have thought or said those words to ourselves or others. Encourage group members to take to heart Katherine's reminder that God doesn't say, "Get over it." God says, "Give it to me."

* As a closing prayer, sit with your palms upward. Invite each person to name one thing they are releasing: "Dear God, I give [fill in the blank] to you."

....

Week Eleven

BEHIND-THE-SCENES VIEW

When Jack and I were in seminary, we had daily chapel services. Once a week a professor would preach. I'll never forget the sermon our beloved New Testament professor preached on Genesis 3:1-9. Dr. Mauser grew up in Nazi Germany, and when he was a little boy, his older brother was conscripted into the Hitler Youth and died in a mountaineering accident. His body wasn't found.

Dr. Mauser told us the story of returning home from school one day and hearing his mother sobbing upstairs in his brother's room. Again and again she cried, "My son, my son, where are you?" With deep emotion, Dr. Mauser then connected the cry of his mother with the anguished cry of God in the garden. There wasn't a dry eye in chapel that day.

More than fifteen years after I heard him preach, I gave Katherine a different narrative with the same punch line: the brokenhearted cry of a parent for a beloved lost child.

EXPLORING THE LEADERSHIP LANDSCAPE

The "where are you" question Katherine offers the group pursues Charissa and Hannah and eventually opens them to speaking the truth about where they're stuck and hiding. Community also plays a role in their movement forward. Mara's openness about "dumping her junk" paves the way for Charissa to lay down her mask and confess her sin. And because Meg demonstrates courage to travel into the wilderness of her grief, Hannah opens some long-sealed boxes from her past as well.

* How have you been inspired by the courage of people in your group?

* Has your role as a leader helped or inhibited your own journey toward freedom? In what ways?

* In talking with the retreat group about self-examination and confession, Katherine offers a personal story about the gift of confession in community (*Sensible Shoes*, pp. 288-89). Do you feel similar freedom to speak from your own experience? If your group hasn't felt like a safe place where you can be authentic, why or why not? Speak with God about what you see.

NAVIGATIONAL TIPS

* As an opening prayer, you could use Genesis 3:1-9 for lectio divina before you discuss your responses to the handout.

* Decide whether it's necessary to talk about the characters this week or whether it's enough to share from your own lives.

* The handout question about tone of voice is one to be mindful of whenever we read a text that includes the Lord speaking. This is one of the benefits of reading Scripture aloud: we're more likely to catch the inflections and assumptions we project onto the text.

Week Twelve

BEHIND-THE-SCENES VIEW

After *Sensible Shoes* was published, I wrote goodbye letters to each of the characters, thanking them for all I had learned from them and offering a benediction for their ongoing journeys. (At that point I had no idea I would be writing sequels!) Here are a few lines from each one.

To Meg: You grew so much throughout this journey, and I'm really proud of you. I guess Hannah's letter to you is really what I wanted to say. Your courage is beautiful.

To Mara: I love your candor and artlessness. I love your generosity of spirit. What's remarkable to me is that you responded to God's invitation to healing and transformation, even when your life circumstances didn't change.

To Charissa: You're a quick learner, and I'm confident you will continue to grow, now that you see some of the ways in which you have been bound. I should have had compassion for you from the very beginning. Life on a pedestal is an awful burden.

To Hannah: I see you beginning to relax and emerge as your true self, and I celebrate that for you. Be well. Be whole. And remember, the flowers are for you.

EXPLORING THE LEADERSHIP LANDSCAPE

* As a blessing to members of your group, consider writing a thank-you letter to each one, identifying the ways you've seen them grow and naming the particular gifts they have given you.

* What kind of letter might Jesus write to you as the leader of the group? What would he specifically thank you for? How would he encourage you? What blessing are you able to receive from him? (Pay attention to any resistance you might feel in imagining such a letter!)

* As a way of blessing your group (or as a group unison blessing), you might speak Katherine's final prayer (*Sensible Shoes*, p. 326) before you read Ephesians 3:20-21 together:

May you grow in the knowledge of God's deep love for you. May you learn to relax into God and rest in his power and faithfulness. May you find opportunities to love God and love others. And since God made us for life together, may you find trustworthy companions to walk with you along the way.

NAVIGATIONAL TIPS

* Emphasize Katherine's words about the importance of flexibility for a rule of life. Not only does a rule take into account seasons of life, but it also considers God-given temperaments. Spiritual disciplines that are life-giving for introverts (e.g., silence and solitude) are more challenging for extroverts, who thrive with corporate disciplines. Some people pray best when they're walking, others when they're sitting. Some connect with God better in spaces without visual distractions, while others connect better while enjoying art or nature. Avoid creating any false hierarchies of holiness when it comes to practicing spiritual disciplines.

* If possible, give a flower to each person in your group. Make sure to give yourself one too.

* Plan an opportunity for celebration together.

* Consider taking a Sensible Shoes retreat together to create time and space for more extended reflection and prayer in community.

PART TWO

Leading Retreats

INTRODUCTION

One day I received an email about a church that had used *Sensible Shoes* as the basis for their weekend women's retreat—unexpectedly. After months of coordinating details with their retreat speaker, the group gathered at the out-of-town venue to discover that the speaker had not arrived. When they contacted her to find out where she was, she confessed she had written down the wrong date and wouldn't be coming. The group panicked. What would they do?

Someone on the planning team spoke up. "I think I have an idea," she said. "Give me until the morning." Then she went to her room and pulled out her copy of *Sensible Shoes*, which she had brought to read during free time at the retreat. The next morning she told the group, "We'll use this."

So they did. Though no one else in the group had read the book, they used the spiritual discipline handouts to frame their individual practice and reflection time and met in small groups for processing and prayer. "It was the best retreat we've ever had," the team member told me. What a beautiful testimony of the Lord's surprising provision!

After years of speaking at retreats and leading others in the practice of spiritual disciplines, I want to provide additional content and resources for you as you create space for drawing near to God, both for in-person and online gatherings. I've also included creative ideas I've heard from many groups that have used *Sensible Shoes* for retreats.

May the Holy Spirit inspire you as you pray, plan, and prepare. And may the Spirit stir and satisfy your longings as you retreat together.

FRAMING EXPECTATIONS

Say the words "women's retreat" and many different images come to mind. For some it means a weekend away to gather with friends, play games, listen to a speaker, and engage in outdoor activities that aren't part of a regular rhythm of life. For others it means getting away for rest, quiet, and prayer. We all have personal definitions of what is life-giving and renewing.

I'll never forget a particular phone call with a member of a retreat planning committee. She had read *Sensible Shoes* and had recommended me as a speaker. Once we discussed the various logistics of the event (dates, cost, venue, theme) and had agreed to move forward, she said, "We've been doing this retreat for twenty years, and it's always the highlight of our women's ministry. We love being together and having fun. So, I have to ask: Are you funny?"

As soon as I recovered from my surprise, I replied, "No, I'm not funny."

She laughed. Nervously. "Well, I mean, I know your books aren't funny, but..."

"No, I'm definitely not funny," I said.

There was a beat of awkward silence before she said, "Oh." In the billowing quiet, I could tell she was trying to figure out how to proceed. So was I.

"Here's what I recommend," I finally said. "Go back to your team, tell them I'm not funny, and then let me know if you still want me to be your speaker."

A few weeks later she phoned again. "We still want you to be our speaker, but we don't want you to come until Saturday morning. That way we can do all our fun and games together on Friday night before you arrive."

I'm so grateful we had the opportunity to clarify our expectations before the event, and I've used that experience in my conversations with other groups since then, as we discern whether my passions and gifts align with their desires and priorities.

Unless someone has had experience with a guided contemplative or silence and solitude retreat, the kind of "sacred journey" retreat described in *Sensible Shoes* might feel foreign and intimidating. Most people aren't accustomed to practicing silence in community, and it can be uncomfortable. Especially when silence provides room for the Holy Spirit to be surgically precise in bringing to the surface what we might prefer to ignore.

Giving time for extended prayer and reflection, however, doesn't mean we can't also give space for recreation and fun. After all, celebration is an important spiritual discipline! Each planning team will need to prayerfully decide how best to practice this in community and then communicate clearly to participants ahead of time what to expect in terms of "fun and games."

THE DIFFERENCE BETWEEN
A CONFERENCE AND A RETREAT

Many of the events I've spoken at have been Saturday or Friday evening/Saturday events, typically hosted by a church. For these events, expectations are naturally different than for an out-of-town weekend retreat. But it's still important to clarify what you intend to offer. Most people are familiar with a conference format: pay a registration fee, hear a keynote speaker (or multiple speakers), and choose from a variety of breakout sessions. The goal of a conference is to provide training and education. The goal of a retreat is to provide space where participants can encounter God. Both are worthy kingdom endeavors.

A conference focuses on supplying information to enhance life, develop skills, or deepen understanding. A retreat focuses on facilitating time with God to deepen relationship with him and experience transformation. This requires space to breathe. When Katherine tells Charissa she won't be distributing a syllabus, Charissa is frustrated. She's expecting a class on spiritual disciplines where she can gain new skills. What she's offered instead is a retreat.

Sensible Shoes provides a gentle on-ramp for exploring the contemplative life, both individually and in community. Many who read *Sensible Shoes* have never heard of the prayer practices that Katherine introduces, and their longings are stirred. I often hear from readers who want to attend the kind of retreat the characters experience but don't know where to go. Conferences that focus on different aspects of spiritual formation are great opportunities for growth. But this guide is designed to help you host a retreat.

FREQUENTLY ASKED QUESTIONS

Do participants need to read **Sensible Shoes** ***before the retreat?*** It's helpful if participants have read *Sensible Shoes* before the retreat so they have an idea of what to expect, but it's not necessary. The retreat is not based on the story or characters in the book, but rather on the spiritual practices. I recommend that everyone on the planning team read the book before the retreat. Ideally, the planning team would commit to using the twelve-week *Sensible Shoes Study Guide* in preparation together. This is a great way to build community and attend to your own sacred journeys before you invite others into the journey.

Are we permitted to make copies of the handouts in **Sensible Shoes** *to distribute at the retreat?* No. But you are welcome to use the handouts for your own presentation notes. If you buy copies of *Sensible Shoes* for your participants, you may print out copies of each of the handouts for free distribution to those participants.

Do we need a trained facilitator or speaker to lead the retreat? No. This guide is designed to help you use Katherine's content in *Sensible Shoes* as a launching point for personal and group reflection. If you have access to someone trained as a retreat leader or spiritual director who can present the content in a more extended teaching time, that's great. But it isn't necessary. If members of your retreat team have personal experience in practicing the disciplines described in the book (even at a "beginner" stage), this is enough to invite others into the practice. Depending on the experience available on your team, you can take turns presenting the content.

How many sessions should we plan? If you're hosting a Friday evening through Sunday morning event, plan for no more than six. If you're hosting a single-day event, plan for no more than three. The priority is to provide plenty of space to breathe and be with God. It would be counterproductive to send people home exhausted from having too much to absorb and process!

What's the ideal group size for a retreat? Much of that will depend on your venue and vision. This guide can be adapted for a large group as well as for a small group of friends gathering for a weekend away.

What if it isn't feasible to gather in the same space? Do online retreats work? They do—very well. This guide includes a section designed for conducting virtual retreats.

PLANNING YOUR RETREAT

Your most important work as a retreat team will be prayer. In addition to practicing prayerful discernment during your planning meetings, leverage the spiritual gifts of people who are passionate and committed to intercession. Not only can intercessors be in prayer for you as you plan the retreat, but they can also be in prayer for participants before, during, and after the retreat. Katherine's prayer before spiritual direction could be a prayer for you to adopt as you meet to plan (*Sensible Shoes*, p. 122):

> Jesus Christ, Light of the World, come and light the dark corners of our lives. Where we are blind, grant us sight. Where we stumble in darkness, illumine our path. Quiet us with your love, and enable us to hear your still, small voice. For you are our dear friend, Lord, and we long to be fully present to you.

I recommend keeping your planning meetings separate from your *Sensible Shoes* small group sessions so you can devote yourselves fully to the spiritual formation journey, individually and in community. This in turn will affect the way you welcome and guide others into retreat.

Once you have decided on a venue, date, and time framework for your retreat, you can begin to ask other questions that will impact your planning and preparation.

* What will you title the retreat?

* Is your retreat only for women?

* Is your retreat intentionally intergenerational? If so, do you have a minimum age requirement, or will participation be dependent on maturity level?

* Is your retreat primarily focused on personal reflection or on building and strengthening bonds of community? Or a combination?

* Is your retreat designed for people from your local church community, or are you hoping to collaborate with other churches and groups for a broader reach?

* If your retreat focuses on building community, will you assign people to small groups or let them choose their own tables for the day or weekend? Will you have designated small group facilitators at each table?

* Will you have a prayer team available for ministry during your retreat? If so, ask them to form a group to study *Sensible Shoes* as well.

* Will you have spiritual directors available during your retreat? If so, how will people register for appointments? Will there be an extra charge?

* Will you have rooms designated for particular spiritual practices (e.g., labyrinth, prayer collage or art, guided journaling)?

* If food is not being provided by your venue, how will you ensure that people with Martha's serving gifts are also able to sit at Jesus' feet and receive? (I've attended some women's events where men cooked, served, and cleaned up in the kitchen—a beautiful gift of service!)

* Will you incorporate music through live singing? If so, how often? Will you play instrumental music during the reflection times or invite people into silence?

* How will you close your retreat? With corporate worship? Large group sharing?

* What do you hope God will do, individually and corporately, during your retreat? What do you hope people will say after the retreat is over?

THE IMPORTANCE OF HOSPITALITY

Jesus speaks of the blessing given to anyone who offers a cup of cold water in his name (Matthew 10:42). As a team, you've committed yourselves to serving others, first by inviting the thirsty to come and then by offering space where they can drink deeply from the water Jesus promises to give.

Creating hospitable space begins before anyone arrives at your event. Think about the courage it took for Meg or Mara to show up at New Hope! From the moment you extend the first invitation to the retreat, watch for ways to offer encouragement and reassurance that this will be an event where all will be warmly welcomed and cared for, whether they come alone or with a group of friends.

The Greek word for hospitality (*philoxenia*) literally means "friend of strangers" or "love of strangers." Hospitality is broader and deeper than the food we serve or the decorations that enhance our physical space, significant as these elements are. Hospitality is also a ministry of helping to remove the obstacles and barriers that keep people from encountering God, others, and themselves in life-transforming ways. There will be people who come to your retreat who feel like a stranger to God, to themselves, and to community. How will you help facilitate a move from stranger to friend?

THE INVITATION

The flyer from New Hope is designed to meet people in their weariness with an invitation to rest:

> Jesus says, "Are you tired? Worn out? Burned out on religion? Come to me. Get away with me and you'll recover your life. I'll show you how to take a real rest. Walk with me and work with me—watch how I do it. Learn the unforced rhythms of grace. I won't lay anything heavy or ill-fitting on you. Keep company with me and you'll learn to live freely and lightly" (Matthew 11:28-30 *The Message*). We invite you to come take a sacred journey."

Many who attend your retreat will be able to answer those first few questions with a yes.

The rest of the New Hope invitation reads, "The sacred journey is a pilgrimage for those who are thirsty for more of God. This journey is for all those who are dissatisfied with living on the surface and who want to travel deeper into God's heart. We invite you to come and explore spiritual disciplines as we seek to create sacred space for God."

This paragraph gives Mara pause (*Sensible Shoes*, p. 34). She doesn't like the word *discipline*. She already feels a weight of shame and guilt about her life and doesn't want more shame and guilt heaped on her. As you pray about what kind of publicity to create, consider how best to communicate clearly what your hopes are for the retreat and what makes this retreat different from other events. Your warm and generous welcome begins here.

Prepare the Way in Prayer

Before their fourth retreat session, Katherine prays alone in the chapel, using words from Isaiah 40:1-3 to frame her longings for the group. Here's part of her prayer: "Clear away any obstacles that hinder your coming into their lives. Meet them in the wilderness of their fear and shame and sorrow and regret. Come, Lord God, and make straight paths for them to travel more deeply into your heart of love" (*Sensible Shoes*, p. 223).

As you pray and plan, are you able to identify any obstacles that can be addressed and removed before the retreat? Anything that might hinder someone from coming away to rest? (Common examples are cost, transportation, and childcare.) How might your wider community help address the obstacles and needs you identify?

Because it can take a bit of time to settle into the rhythm of a day or two away, you might create a pre-retreat guide with key Scriptures, prayers, or *Sensible Shoes* quotes, as well as reminders of what to bring (and not to bring!) to help prepare the way. Email this to participants the week before.

You can adapt and use Katherine's prayer for your planning sessions, asking God to remove obstacles and make straight paths for people to travel more deeply into his love. Once you begin to assemble your list of guests, you or the intercessory prayer team can pray for each by name.

Make Yourselves at Home

Jesus says, "As the Father has loved me, so I have loved you; abide in my love" (John 15:9). In *The Message* Eugene Peterson renders that last phrase as, "Make yourselves at home in my love." What a beautiful invitation and image to ponder. How will you best communicate that kind of welcome to all who arrive? Here are some suggestions:

* Design a welcome pack or folder. (Sample content is provided on pp. 69-70.)
* Since guests will arrive with a variety of stress levels, burdens, and needs, appoint people with gifts of hospitality, encouragement, and even pastoral care to serve at your welcome/registration table.

* Establish the physical atmosphere from the first point of contact in the space. It doesn't need to be expensive or complicated decor. Focus on simple ways to put people at ease and make them feel valued and at home the moment they arrive.

* Decide how best to communicate warmth and welcome, even through the positioning of chairs in your large group meeting space. Will you be in rows? Around tables?

* If you will be using multiple designated spaces for prayer and reflection, supply information in your welcome packet, including room numbers, a description for each room, and instructions about when the rooms will be open for use. Don't forget to create spaces that are set apart for silence as well as spaces that are open for conversation and socializing. It will be important to communicate "protocol" for each space (including your primary meeting area) throughout the retreat.

* If your venue is not supplying meals, decide what kind of food you will provide and how frequently. What do you want to communicate through what you offer? What kind of accommodations are you able to make for people with food allergies or sensitivities?

* Be creative in weaving visual themes into your retreat. Some groups supply homemade notebooks decorated with maps or shoes. Others provide shoe-themed treats. (I've attended events with shoe-shaped chocolates and cookies, as well as high heel cupcakes—not very "sensible," but delicious.) Some groups use shoes to create table centerpieces or to decorate a stage. The theme of "the flowers are for you" can also be easily incorporated into decor, food, and giveaways.

RETREAT CONTENT OVERVIEW

In this section you'll find summaries of the prayer practices and spiritual disciplines the characters explore during their retreat in *Sensible Shoes*. I've also included tips for leading others in the engagement of these disciplines. Feel free to select the ones that will best serve your group during your allotted time.

Welcome

Designate someone to offer the welcome (including announcements, rhythm for the day, etc.). Remind people to turn off their cell phones (and give the reminder before each session). If you are including small group conversation during your retreat, speak about the importance of confidentiality as a gift you give one another (see the introduction to part one in this guide as well as p. 10 in the *Sensible Shoes Study Guide*). We ask God for the grace of compassion, not only for ourselves during retreat but for our traveling companions.

As part of the opening prayer, you may wish to include one of the texts Katherine uses to extend an invitation to retreat. After you read the text, allow a few moments for quiet prayer. If you are gathered around tables, you might then ask people to introduce themselves and share one hope they have for the retreat.

> Jesus says, "Are you tired? Worn out? Burned out on religion? Come to me. Get away with me and you'll recover your life. I'll show you how to take a real rest. Walk with me and work with me—watch how I do it. Learn the unforced rhythms of grace. I won't lay anything heavy or ill-fitting on you. Keep company with me and you'll learn to live freely and lightly." (Matthew 11:28-30 *The Message*)

> Blessed are those whose strength is in you,
>   whose hearts are set on pilgrimage.
> As they pass through the Valley of Baka,
>   they make it a place of springs;
>   the autumn rains also cover it with pools.

They go from strength to strength,
   till each appears before God in Zion. (Psalm 84:5-7 NIV)

OPENING PRAYER EXERCISES

Several of the disciplines the characters learn are well-suited for use at the beginning of a session as a way of centering in the presence of God. Before you present the content of your opening session, you could teach one of these prayers and give a few minutes to practice in silence.

Palms up, palms down (**Sensible Shoes, pp. 180-81**). Katherine invites the group to practice releasing and receiving with open hands. (I learned this prayer method from author Richard Foster.) Invite the group to begin by making tight fists. Feel the clench and tension in your body. Then open your hands and feel the release of tension. Note that we both release and receive with open hands.

With your palms face-down, release to God the things that distract and weigh you down. Silently name anything that comes to mind. When you're ready, turn your palms face-up to receive God's gifts to you. As often as you need to, turn your palms over and back again to release and receive.

This prayer practice matches well with 1 Peter 5:7: "Cast all your anxiety on him, because he cares for you." It also matches well with the invitation from Matthew 11:28-30 to exchange our heavy yokes and burdens for Jesus' light yoke and rest.

Breath prayer (p. 64). Katherine offers Meg her favorite breath prayer, based on 2 Corinthians 12:9. "I can't" (inhale). "You can, Lord" (exhale). Practicing breath prayer is a beautiful way to pray continually (1 Thessalonians 5:17) as we match the rhythm of our breathing with the cries and longings of our hearts. There's no right or wrong way to do it. You might choose a short verse and divide it into an inhale/exhale pattern, such as, "Be still and know" (inhale) "that I am God" (exhale) (Psalm 46:10). Or choose a name for God from Scripture and then express a brief declaration of faith, petition, or desire. Example: "Emmanuel" (inhale), "you are with me" (exhale).

Offer your group a few minutes of silence to listen for a prayer. How is God inviting you to know and name him? What does God invite you to declare about who he is and what you need? (Reassure perfectionists that they don't need to find the perfect prayer—just something simple that matches their longings or needs.) After giving a few minutes to find a prayer, give more silence to pray with it. As you breathe, receive the very Breath of God. (Both the Hebrew and Greek words for "breath" also mean "spirit.") Practice being attentive to your breathing throughout the day and in the coming days so that prayer becomes more habitual.

Personalizing Scripture (p. 149). Katherine suggests that Meg insert her own name into a Scripture text for prayer as a way of meditating on God's love, presence, and power. While Meg uses Isaiah 43:1-2 for prayer, any text that addresses the people of God can be prayed in this way. Pick a verse that offers an invitation to you as you gather, then supply the words via a screen or handout for silent prayer.

Here are two examples. By leaving the plural references unchanged, we remind ourselves that while the call is deeply personal, it's given to us in community.

Stand at the crossroads, [insert name], and look,
   and ask for the ancient paths,
where the good way lies; and walk in it, [insert name],
   and find rest for your souls. (Jeremiah 6:16)

Come to me, all you that are weary and are carrying heavy burdens, and I will give you rest, [insert name]. Take my yoke upon you, [insert name], and learn from me; for I am gentle and humble in heart, and you will find rest for your souls. For my yoke is easy, [insert name], and my burden is light. (Matthew 11:28-30)

OPENING SESSION

Before you present your first spiritual discipline, it will be helpful to give a brief overview. Here's an introduction you can use or adapt.

For many people, the phrase "spiritual discipline" conjures up images of drudgery, guilt, or obligation. What we need is a paradigm shift. Spiritual disciplines are ways to practice being attentive to the God who is always attentive to us. Spiritual disciplines are ways to practice being awake to the presence of God. Spiritual disciplines are ways to practice receiving the love of God, resting in the love of God, and responding to the love of God. They aren't rules to follow but ways to practice deepening our intimacy with God and cooperating with the Spirit's work in our lives. (See *Sensible Shoes*, pp. 33-35, 50-53 for the ways Dawn and Katherine speak about spiritual disciplines.)

If we look at the life of Jesus, we see many spiritual disciplines he practiced: worship, reading and meditating on God's Word, prayer, fasting, silence, solitude, discernment, retreat, serving, simplicity, lament, sacrifice, fellowship, submission, and celebration. If these habits and practices shaped Jesus' life, how much more are we invited to practice listening and responding to God?

Spiritual disciplines are both individual and corporate. Introverts will gravitate toward practices of silence and solitude, while extroverts will gravitate toward practices of community. Both kinds are essential in our spiritual formation. We need to let go of any idea of a "holiness hierarchy" when it comes to life with God and instead embrace the reality that God has designed us with unique temperaments and gifts. Some pray best in quiet and stillness. Some pray best while walking. Some are most aware of God's presence in corporate worship or through music. Others are awake to God's presence in nature or when immersed in beauty.

During this retreat we invite you into the practice of some spiritual disciplines that have been part of Christian life and community for centuries, even millennia. Wherever you are today, whether familiar with these practices or not, we pray that you will encounter God in significant ways as together we say yes to dwelling more deeply in his love and to being enlarged to love God and others more deeply in return.

[Introduce the first spiritual discipline.]

SPIRITUAL DISCIPLINES

∽

1 LABYRINTH

(Sensible Shoes, pp. 53-62, 94-97, 129-32, 175-77, 327-28)

In the book Katherine uses the labyrinth for their first session to introduce the group to the imagery of a pilgrimage. Because the labyrinth incorporates disciplines of slowing down, silence, and prayer, it provides a good entry point for retreat.

Some retreat centers and churches have outdoor labyrinths or canvas labyrinths that can be used indoors. (Some organizations also rent out canvas labyrinths.) If you are planning to use the labyrinth as one of your retreat sessions, here are some logistics to consider, as well as practical tips.

* Keep in mind that the New Hope retreat group had less than twenty-five people, and participants still had to take turns. Count on at least thirty to forty minutes to walk a traditional eleven-circuit labyrinth, like the Chartres Cathedral design (*Sensible Shoes*, p. 55). Depending on the size of your group and the size of the labyrinth, you may need to divide into smaller groups for access. This means allowing more time for the session.

* If you need to divide your group, provide other resources such as guided reflection questions or access to designated creative prayer spaces while people wait their turn. Be sure to give adequate space for reflection after walking the labyrinth so that people can process what they experienced. You can decide if you will incorporate group sharing time as well.

* Rather than using the labyrinth as a session, you could offer it as a prayer opportunity during any of the reflection times. This would then become one of your designated prayer spaces.

* Labyrinths are expensive to purchase and can be complicated to make. I've attended many retreats with simplified labyrinths outlined in

masking tape on carpet or ropes on grass. They don't have to be fancy— just a simple pattern that can be walked slowly in prayer.

* When walking a labyrinth isn't possible, finger labyrinths can be a creative way to slow down, ponder, and pray. (See the prayer cards, as well as examples at the Shepherd's Corner website, https://shepherdscorner .org/2020/03/25/finger-labyrinths-for-meditation.)

* Some people are comforted by specific instructions. Though there is no right or wrong way to walk and pray a labyrinth, you could provide Scripture verses to meditate on or short prayers for a journey.

* As you introduce the labyrinth, draw from Katherine's teaching (*Sensible Shoes*, pp. 53-55) and the brief overview provided in part one of this guide (pp. 20-21). You can also incorporate my words about Christian freedom (*Sensible Shoes Study Guide*, p. 20).

2 Lectio Divina

(Sensible Shoes, pp. 102-7, 134-36, 195-97)

Lectio divina (pronounced "LEC-tsee-o" or "LEC-tee-o" "di-VEE-na") is an ancient way of meditating on Scripture, dating to the sixth century. In the twelfth century lectio divina became more formalized into a four-step rhythm.

* *Lectio:* We read God's Word slowly, prayerfully, and attentively, listening for the Spirit to bring to life a word or phrase from the text.

* *Meditatio:* We chew on a word or phrase from God's Word, pondering how it addresses us or intersects with our lives.

* *Oratio:* We savor God's Word and respond to what the Spirit brings to life by having a conversation with God.

* *Contemplatio:* We rest in the presence of God in silence.

Since it is easy to become distracted by the "dance steps" of lectio divina, I recommend leading the prayer from the front, with silence between each reading and extended time of prayer and reflection after the exercise. Plan on fifteen to twenty minutes of guided prayer, followed by at least thirty minutes of silence and solitude.

Lectio divina is a prayer practice that can dramatically impact the way we read and receive God's Word, both individually and in community. When I lead retreats on spiritual disciplines, I always include lectio divina as one of the main sessions. Since the Spirit brings the Word to life in unique ways, it's a gift to also engage in small or large group conversation about what we noticed as we prayed with God's Word. (Allow at least thirty minutes for group interaction.)

The rhythm I offer in *Sensible Shoes* is for corporate lectio divina. But you might also provide instructions for how to practice it individually.

For personal practice

* Choose a short passage of Scripture, no more than a few verses, especially if those verses are densely packed. If I'm praying with Psalm 23, for example, I might read only the first two verses. And I might read the same text several days.

* Read the verses aloud. Reading aloud not only slows us down but helps us receive the Word in multiple ways.

* Listen for a word or phrase from the text that catches your attention—something that shimmers or comes into bold print. You might need to read the text several times before anything catches your attention. If, however, a word or phrase addresses you on your first or second reading, stop there and begin to chew on it.

* Ponder what connections the word has with your life. Note any thoughts or feelings that arise around this word or phrase. Then talk with God about what you notice. Listen for God's invitations and call. Consider how God is calling you to respond to his Word. Conclude your time of prayer by resting in God's presence in wordless prayer.

* If nothing comes into bold print for you as you read and pray, trust that the Word has still descended from your mind to your heart, where it will take root and shape and form you. You may even discover it pursues you long after you finish your time of prayer.

For large group presentation

In addition to the content in *Sensible Shoes*, tips for leading a group in lectio divina are provided on pages 25-26 of this guide. Here are some other suggestions for presenting this discipline during your retreat.

* Read from the handout on page 102 or adapt it into your own words, noting how we often read God's Word for information rather than transformation. Extend an invitation to listen to God's Word in a different way.

* Give some examples of how you or your team have been shaped by this way of prayer, individually and in community. If you offer stories about certain texts coming to life for you, avoid sharing details about the text you will be offering for prayer at the retreat. (For example, don't talk about how you prayed with John 1:35-39 if this will be your text.)

* Choose a short text from Scripture that is well-suited for your hopes, longings, or theme for your retreat.

* Ask the group not to open Bibles to follow along as you read but instead focus on listening to the Word. Supply the Scripture reference before you begin so they can continue to pray with the text during the reflection time. If necessary, provide a few words of context for the passage. (For John 1:35-39, you might say that the story takes place after Jesus' baptism, and the "John" mentioned is John the Baptist, not John the disciple.)

* Tell the group that you will read the text four times, with silence after each reading, and that you will guide them through the exercise so they don't have to worry about what to do next.

* Let the group know that you will read the text as neutrally as possible, without emphasizing certain words or phrases, so as not to distract or influence their hearing.

* Reassure the group that it's fine if several different words or phrases catch their attention as they listen (or if a different word or phrase comes to life after each reading). Just let it all settle into prayer. If no word or phrase catches their attention, they can speak with God about this as well.

[Note: Katherine invites the group to listen for a word or phrase that catches their attention during the first reading. But I've found it helps to let the first reading be an opportunity simply to listen to the overall movement of the text. This gives a bit of extra time to settle into hearing the Word.]

Here's a template you can use or adapt:

1. Before you read the text the first time, invite the group to take a posture of prayer that reminds them they are in the presence of the One who knows them and loves them. Allow a moment of quiet centering in God's presence. Then say, "For this opening reading of the Scripture text, listen to the overall movement of it. Ask the Lord for the grace to hear it as if you're hearing it for the very first time. Try not to analyze it. Just receive it and ask the Holy Spirit to bring it to life for you." Give a few moments of silence. Then read the text. Allow one or two minutes of silence after you read the text.

2. Before you read the text a second time, say, "As you hear the Scripture a second time, listen for a word or phrase that seems to choose you, something that comes into bolder print than the rest. Don't strive to figure out which word or phrase that is. Just receive whatever comes." Give a moment of silence, then read the text. After you read, give a few moments of silence. Then say, "If a word or phrase has come into bold print for you, linger with it. What thoughts, feelings, or memories arise in you as you hold this word or phrase? How does this word or phrase intersect with your life right now?" Give a few minutes of silence for prayerful pondering.

3. Read the text a third time. After you read, give a moment of silence. Then say, "Talk honestly with God about whatever you're noticing, and listen for God's invitations to you. How are you being called to respond to God's Word? What do you need from God right now?" Give at least five minutes for silent prayer.

4. Read the text a fourth time. After you read, give a moment of silence. Then say, "In the quiet, rest in the presence of God. No words are necessary. Just enjoy this place of communion with the God who loves you." Give one to two minutes of silence. Then close your time of prayer (e.g., "In Jesus' name we pray, Amen").

5. Give a moment of silence for people to emerge from this time of reflection. Then offer your next instructions to the group. Ask them to hold silence for the next half an hour (or longer). Invite them to spread out and go to whichever space will best serve them as they continue in quiet reflection and response to God's Word. Let them know what time to return for small group conversation or for your next presentation.

3 PRAYER OF EXAMEN

(Sensible Shoes, pp. 178-83, 193-94, 198, 253-54)

The prayer of examen (pronounced "ig-ZAY-men") is typically practiced at the end of the day, so it is well-suited as a final session, especially for a day-long retreat. It does not need to be a long prayer. For people who are practiced in it, the prayer might be a ten- to fifteen-minute review of the day. For those who are new to the discipline, it's good to have more time. I recommend giving at least forty-five minutes of personal reflection time after the presentation of the examen. If participants don't need that much time with it, they can make use of the silence and solitude for further reflection on the day. Or they can use the examen to prayerfully review a larger stretch of time—not just weeks or months, but also seasons of life that have not yet been prayerfully processed. Some people divide their lives into seven-year segments, beginning in early childhood, and use the examen questions to watch for patterns. (If you are doing a weekend event, this kind of exercise blends well with the "wilderness questions.")

Another option is to incorporate the prayer of examen at the end of your retreat day as a final prayer. Instead of teaching it and giving extended time to practice, you can lead the prayer from the front, giving silent space for reflection after each movement of the prayer. (See template below.)

In addition to the content provided on the examen handout and in Katherine's teaching, here are some suggestions for how to present the examen to your group.

* Affirm the challenges of being awake and attentive to the presence of God. Identify some of the elements that hinder and distract us. Acknowledge that some of us are fearful about what we might see if we pay

attention. Offer reassurance about the goodness and love of God, who does not reveal the truth to punish us but to set us free.

* Weave in personal examples of what you have noticed as you have practiced praying the examen. (With your team's permission and/or participation, speak about how you have practiced this in community and what you have noticed together.) Model vulnerability. Name the fruit of this practice as a way of encouraging others.

* Note that the things that catch our attention as we pray can seem very ordinary, even inconsequential. But if we are willing to listen, we may discover the Spirit revealing something that surprises us.

* Emphasize that the examen is prayer. It's a conversation with God. It's not self-scrutiny for the sake of self-improvement. It's a humble and hopeful prayer: "Search me and know me and reveal what I need to see so that I may become more attentive to your presence, more aware of your love, and more fully the person you have created me to be."

* Encourage the group to keep track of what they notice, through journaling or list making or doodling. Recording what we notice helps us see patterns and themes emerge.

* Bring to the examen a posture of curiosity, not self-condemnation.

Before you begin your time of prayer, read Psalm 139, even the uncomfortable section (vv. 19-22). It all belongs in prayer.

Part of the beauty of the examen is its breathability. The questions presented on the handout are simply suggestions for identifying our soul's movement toward and away from God. Many families are already practiced with this kind of conversation. We often ask children, "What's the best thing that happened to you today? What's the hardest thing that happened to you today?" These questions lie at the heart of the examen. But rather than simply engaging conversation with one another, we bring the conversation into our life with God, individually and in community.

Here's a corporate examen template:

1. We take time to silently express our gratitude to God for the gifts of the day. (2 minutes)

2. We ask the Lord to search us and know us (Psalm 139:23-24) and make us attentive to what he wants us to see. (1 minute)

3. We prayerfully scan our day, looking for moments when we were aware of the presence of God, when we moved toward God, when we were brought to life with joy or peace or hope, when we were enabled to love God and others, and when we received God's comfort. We take time to notice, celebrate, and give thanks for these gifts. (5-7 minutes)

4. We prayerfully scan our day, looking for moments when we were not aware of the presence of God, when God seemed hidden, when we resisted moving toward God, when we were discouraged or fearful or agitated, when we turned aside from loving God and loving others. We take time to notice and grieve what needs to be grieved. We name our need for God and receive his comfort. We confess our sins and receive God's grace and forgiveness. (5-7 minutes)

5. We look forward with hope. In light of what we have noticed from our life with God today, how can we live tomorrow differently? How might we practice being more attentive to the presence and movement of the Holy Spirit in our lives? (3-5 minutes)

If desired, this corporate examen can be followed by a time of group discussion.

4 WILDERNESS QUESTIONS

(Sensible Shoes, pp. 224-30, 236-41)

Where have you come from? Where are you going?

Katherine offers these probing questions at the beginning of their fourth session, as a midpoint reflection on the journey. Since the New Hope retreat takes place over several months, the participants have by this time had adequate space to practice being attentive to God's presence and to process some of the ways God has met them in the wilderness seasons of loss, sorrow, and transition.

Note how carefully and tenderly Katherine guides the group before they contemplate these deep heart questions. For these reasons, I don't recommend offering the wilderness questions as a separate session (especially during a single-day retreat). Instead, these questions could be incorporated into a creative space as an option for journaling and prayer. If you will be giving extended time to the prayer of examen during a weekend event, these questions could be incorporated as part of discerning God's presence in the past and guidance for the present and future.

5 PRAYING WITH IMAGINATION

(Sensible Shoes, pp. 48-49, 96-98, 242-48)

Katherine opens their first session with a brief exercise of praying with imagination, inviting participants to imagine themselves with Jesus as he calls his first disciples to follow him (Mark 1:16-20). Her instructions are simple: Listen to the story. Imagine you are there. What do you see? Hear? Feel? Where are you in the story? Then talk with God about whatever you notice (p. 48). During their fourth session, when she introduces this discipline for a more extended time of prayer, she not only supplies more specifics but also acknowledges her own initial reluctance to pray this way (pp. 242-45). I share this in common with Katherine (see the leader's notes to week nine in this guide).

Because praying with imagination can be uncomfortable and foreign for some, it helps to name the challenges and to offer examples of your or your team's experience with this discipline. Like lectio divina, this is a discipline of prayer—not Bible study—and is a rich and fascinating one to practice in community, as each person will have a different experience praying with the text.

Some will embrace this discipline wholeheartedly, without hesitation. Since others might need additional help, I've provided two guided reflections below. You are free to write your own guide for whichever passage you choose, but offer only one Scripture text to the whole group. I recommend choosing a narrative text from any of the Gospels.

After you present the discipline, read the story to the group a couple of times. Then invite them to pray with it in silence and solitude. (Give at least thirty minutes for this.) They are welcome to spread out into any area that will help them lean into this way of prayer. Let them know when to return. Then give time for small group sharing (at least thirty minutes). During the small group, participants can share either specifics of how the story came to life or challenges they experienced in trying to pray this way.

Praying with John 1:35-39

The next day John again was standing with two of his disciples, and as he watched Jesus walk by, he exclaimed, "Look, here is the Lamb of God!" The two disciples heard him say this, and they followed Jesus. When Jesus turned and saw them following, he said to them, "What are you looking for?" They said to him, "Rabbi" (which translated means Teacher), "where are you staying?" He said to them, "Come and see." They came and saw where he was staying, and they remained with him that day. It was about four o'clock in the afternoon.

1. Imagine the scene. What is the landscape like? What do you see? Hear? Smell? Touch?

2. Where do you find yourself in this story? (For example, are you John the Baptist, pointing others to Jesus? Are you one of the disciples, feeling attracted to following Jesus?) What feelings stir in you as you imagine yourself participating in the story?

3. Jesus turns, looks at you, and asks, "What are you looking for?" With what tone of voice do you imagine Jesus asking the question? How do you answer?

4. How do you feel about staying with Jesus for a while? What obstacles keep you from staying with him?

5. Jesus invites you to "come and see." What would you like to see when you're with Jesus? Is there anything you are afraid you might see while you're with him?

6. What would you like to say to God in response to what you're noticing right now?

Praying with Luke 5:1-5

(Note: Deliberately leave the text in tension. If you know the end of the story, try to set the ending aside as you enter this text with your imagination.)

Once while Jesus was standing beside the lake of Gennesaret, and the crowd was pressing in on him to hear the word of God, he saw two boats there at the shore of the lake; the fishermen had gone out of them and were washing their nets. He got into one of the boats, the one belonging to Simon, and asked him to put out a little way from the shore. Then he sat down and taught the crowds from the boat. When he had finished speaking, he said to Simon, "Put out into the deep water and let down your nets for a catch." Simon answered, "Master, we have worked all night long but have caught nothing. Yet if you say so, I will let down the nets."

1. Picture the scene—the land, the crowds, the sea, the boats, the chores, the conversations. Where are you in the scene? What do you see? Hear? Smell? Touch? Taste? What thoughts and feelings arise in you as you participate in the story? Are you watching and listening to Jesus, or is your attention diverted elsewhere?

2. Now imagine you are Simon Peter. How do you feel when Jesus asks to use your boat? How do you feel when he commands you to go out into the deep water and lower your nets? Use all of your senses as you consider what thoughts and feelings might arise after a night of fruitless labor.

3. Imagine offering Simon Peter's objection to Jesus: "Master, we have worked all night long but have caught nothing." Stay awhile with your objection before you move to obedience. What thoughts and feelings arise as you offer your resistance to him? With what tone of voice do you speak your objection?

4. Now imagine moving toward saying, "Yet if you say so, I will let down the nets." How much time passes between offering your objection and offering your obedience? With what tone of voice do you speak the words, "Yet if you say so . . ."?

5. What do you imagine Jesus' facial expressions to be during this exchange? What does this reveal about how you see Jesus? Yourself?

6. How comfortable are you in offering objections and resistance to Jesus' commands? If you hesitate to express yourself freely to him, why might this be?

7. What do you hope will happen if you obey Jesus? What do these hopes reveal about where you find yourself with God right now? Offer what you've noticed to God in prayer.

6 Self-Examination and Confession

(Sensible Shoes, pp. 137, 162-65, 237-38, 248-50, 288-96, 309-10, 325)

Though Katherine teaches about self-examination and confession during their fifth meeting, the characters practice these disciplines throughout the book. If you plan to present this as a session, it's imperative to ground your group in the love and grace of God first. We will be reluctant to ask God to reveal our sins unless we are confident he will generously forgive our sins when we turn to him to confess.

Depending on the maturity level of your group, you may need to provide teaching on this important topic before you present the Genesis 3 questions for prayer and reflection. It's difficult (though not impossible) to present this session during a one-day (three-session) retreat, as you would first need to lay a significant foundation of trust. If you use it for a weekend event, I recommend teaching the examen in an earlier session. You might then use this as your Saturday evening session, followed by a participatory and creative experience in community to "dump the junk," as Mara says, and celebrate the freedom God gives. Some groups use sandpits for writing sins and erasing them. Others write sins on slips of paper to lay at the foot of a cross or to toss into a bonfire. Community conversation about sin, self-examination, and confession can be deeply healing and transformational when done with compassion and solidarity. (A reminder about your commitment to confidentiality and grace for one another is essential for this session.)

7 Rule of Life

(Sensible Shoes, pp. 319-25)

As with the wilderness questions, the rule of life session is best offered after a more extended time of retreat. If you are hosting a weekend event, this could be your final session. But I don't recommend using it as a final session for a one-day retreat. People need exposure to multiple spiritual disciplines, with ample time to practice them, before being able to discern what brings them to life and how God is inviting them to be stretched and formed by new practices.

In addition to presenting the content from the rule of life handout, weave in Katherine's teaching about the importance of a rule of life being flexible and adaptable, well-suited for seasons of life and temperament (see week twelve tips in part one of this guide). Encourage participants to consider the disciplines they already incorporate into their lives, perhaps so habitually that they aren't even aware they are practicing a discipline (praying before a meal, worshiping in community, studying the Bible, serving, tithing, etc.).

The questions listed on the rule of life handout are helpful to ponder before crafting a rule. Here's additional guidance to offer your group: "Reflect on this particular season of your life. Consider your opportunities and limitations, your roles and responsibilities. In light of these realities and rhythms, identify some spiritual disciplines you believe God is inviting you to practice daily, weekly, monthly, and yearly. Keep in mind both individual and corporate practices. What fruit of these disciplines do you hope you will see as you say yes to God's invitations?"

Encourage people not to add too many new disciplines so as not to grow discouraged. Instead, identify some practices that are already life-giving as well as one or two that are new. As you craft your rules of life, be creative. Use colored pens or pencils. Draw pictures. Use magazine photos to create a collage (if this is life-giving). You might organize it by theme and longings or by listing daily, weekly, monthly, and yearly practices.

Decide whether you will offer an opportunity to share your rules of life in small groups. I recommend allowing at least forty-five minutes for personal reflection after the presentation of the discipline.

RETREAT FOLDER

Welcome

In addition to expressing your gratitude to each person who has come to your retreat, include suggestions for how to settle into the space.

* Give yourself time to arrive. Your mind may be busy with thoughts and worries from where you've come from. Take time to do what you need to do, whether that's finding a quiet corner, walking the grounds, or enjoying a cup of coffee with a friend.

* Take in your surroundings. What catches your attention and reminds you that the Lord is with you in this place?

* Practice the discipline of "unplugging" while you are here. Keep your devices turned off as much as possible so that you can be fully present to God, yourself, and others who have joined you on retreat.

* Commit to being gentle with yourself. Whatever you notice during your journey on retreat, receive it with compassionate curiosity. Try not to judge yourself. We are all in need of mercy in some way, and it is this very need that opens us up to the love and grace of God.

Map (If Necessary)

Remember to include room numbers for any designated prayer spaces.

Schedule for the Retreat

While it's helpful to provide this information (especially if your mealtimes are set by your venue), let your time together breathe. Let people know that you will adjust start and end times of sessions in order to say yes to the Spirit's leading and work.

Sacred Spaces

Identify the spaces that have been set apart for silence and solitude, as well as any special rooms for guided prayer and reflection.

* labyrinth

* creative prayer: coloring, drawing, prayer collage (supply materials for each of these)

  For a weekend retreat, this room can include times for community conversation. But if it is open for people to use during the personal reflection time following a session, it should remain silent for that period.

* journaling

  Provide visual prompts: photos, art, or other evocative objects such as keys, shells, or stones with words printed on them. Be creative! You can also supply questions that invite reflection.

* intercessory prayer

  Identify the times when prayer partners will be available in this room.

Etiquette for Spaces

Establish the priority of holding silence together during reflection times. If possible, keep your main meeting space as a quiet space during your retreat (apart from guided small group conversations). Designate other spaces where people are welcome to socialize during breaks in the day or during extended free time. It's important to honor and accommodate both introverts and extroverts so that all feel seen and welcomed.

Other Pages

Include blank pages for notes in case someone forgets to bring a journal. You might also include theme Scripture verses or favorite *Sensible Shoes* quotes.

ONLINE RETREATS

The year 2020 introduced many of us to online opportunities we had never imagined. When my in-person retreats were canceled, I was initially hesitant about offering online events. What if technology didn't cooperate? What if the disembodied nature of it was too distracting? What if people, for whatever reason, weren't able to enter deeply into the presence of God and experience his rest?

To my surprise, I discovered I loved leading online events. I was also continually reminded that the Holy Spirit meets us just as reliably and faithfully online as he does in person. Yes, hosting an online retreat presents challenges. But it also provides abundant opportunities. What a gift to be unhindered by distance, able to gather from all over the world around a common purpose. Online retreats are also a hospitable option for those who struggle with health issues, disabilities, cost, or social anxiety.

As you plan the timing and content of your sessions for an online retreat, be aware of screen fatigue. I recommend planning an event no longer than five hours, with plenty of space for off-screen personal reflection.

GETTING READY: RESOURCES FOR PARTICIPANTS

Practicing a retreat day at home can be a challenge for many different reasons. Before your retreat, send participants your schedule, along with practical suggestions for creating and protecting sacred space. Here are some recommendations:

* Have an honest conversation with members of your household about what you will need in order to carve out time for silence and solitude. Ask for their help in protecting this space.

* Remove and silence all distractions (devices, phones, etc.).

* Set up a room or corner as designated "sacred space." In addition to your Bible and journal, surround yourself with items that will help center you or bring you joy: a candle or incense, a photograph, a cross,

a fountain, flowers or a potted plant, pen/crayons/colored pencils, an item with special significance, food and drink you will enjoy, magazines/scissors/glue/construction paper for a prayer collage. Make it a hospitable space that will be life-giving to you.

Jesus says, "Are you tired? Worn out? Burned out on religion? Come to me. Get away with me and you'll recover your life. I'll show you how to take a real rest. Walk with me and work with me—watch how I do it. Learn the unforced rhythms of grace. I won't lay anything heavy or ill-fitting on you. Keep company with me and you'll learn to live freely and lightly." (Matthew 11:28-30 *The Message*)

* Write an RSVP note to Jesus' invitation, naming the reasons why you are excited or why you aren't sure about accepting. Speak honestly with God about your longings and fears before your day of retreat. What one thing do you hope you'll be able to say when the retreat is over?

CREATING HOSPITABLE SPACE ONLINE

* If you have access to a team gifted in using technology, leverage their gifts for designing soothing visual graphics for your welcome and invitations to reflection. The screen could show either still photos or moving images. Prayer prompts, reflection questions, or reminders about how to engage with God could be provided on the screen during reflection times. Also include the start time for your next session.

* Open your online platform half an hour before your event begins so participants can log on, chat with one another, and make sure there aren't technical issues to resolve.

* During your presentation times, mute participants and show only the presenter on screen. Decide if you will offer small or large group interaction at designated times during your retreat and explain to people how this will work.

* Designate a point person for any technical difficulties that might arise during the retreat.

SAMPLE SCHEDULES

One-Day Retreat

8:30-9:00 a.m. ~ Registration and coffee

9:00-9:20 a.m. ~ Welcome (includes worship and/or opening prayer exercise)

9:20-9:45 a.m. ~ Session one (spiritual disciplines overview, labyrinth, or praying with imagination)

9:45-10:30 a.m. ~ Personal reflection time (silence and solitude)

10:30-10:45 a.m. ~ Coffee break

10:45-11:30 a.m. ~ Session two (lectio divina)

11:30-12:00 ~ Personal reflection time (silence and solitude)

12:00-12:30 p.m. ~ Small group conversation (or ongoing reflection time)

12:30-1:15 p.m. ~ Lunch (can include guided conversation around tables, sharing "aha" moments)

1:15-1:45 p.m. ~ Session three (prayer of examen)

1:45-2:30 p.m. ~ Personal reflection (silence and solitude)

2:30-2:45 p.m. ~ Coffee break

2:45-3:30 p.m. ~ Small group conversation (or ongoing reflection time)

3:30-4:00 p.m. ~ Closing prayer, worship, or large group reflection

Weekend Retreat

Friday

[Arrival and gathering time]

7:00 p.m. ~ Welcome and opening session

7:50-8:30 p.m. ~ Personal reflection (silence and solitude)

8:30-9:15 p.m. ~ Small group conversation

9:15 p.m. ~ Group or personal activity options

Saturday

[Morning options, breakfast]

9:00 a.m. ~ Session two (can include worship and prayer exercise)

9:45-10:30 a.m. ~ Personal reflection (silence and solitude)

10:30-10:45 a.m. ~ Coffee break

10:45-11:30 a.m. ~ Small group conversation

11:30 a.m. ~ Free time and lunch

1:00 p.m. ~ Session three

1:45-2:30 p.m. ~ Personal reflection (silence and solitude)

2:30-3:00 p.m. ~ Small group conversation

3:00 p.m. until dinner ~ Free time

7:00 p.m. ~ Session four

7:45-8:30 p.m. ~ Personal reflection (silence and solitude)

8:30-9:15 p.m. ~ Small group conversation

9:15 p.m. ~ Evening activities

Sunday

[Morning activities]

9:00 a.m. ~ Closing worship or session five (incorporate personal reflection and/or group conversation according to your finish time)

Online Retreat

8:30-9:00 a.m. ~ Gathering time (chat function is open for people to interact with one another and to communicate any technical difficulties)

9:00-9:15 a.m. ~ Welcome and opening prayer (Include instructions and notes about the technology platform and how group interaction will happen during the day.)

9:15-9:50 a.m. ~ Session one (I recommend using the brief introduction to spiritual disciplines, followed by lectio divina.)

9:50-10:30 a.m. ~ Personal prayer and reflection (Encourage participants to step away from their screens during this time.)

10:30-11:00 a.m. ~ Small groups in chat rooms to share insights (If you will not be offering small group interaction, personal prayer and reflection time can continue.)

11:00-11:30 a.m. ~ Session two (I recommend praying with imagination. You can supply the guided questions for either John 1:35-39 or Luke 5:1-5 verbally and/or onscreen.)

11:30-12:15 p.m. ~ Personal prayer and reflection (includes lunch break)

12:15-12:35 p.m. ~ Small groups in chat rooms or ongoing personal reflection time

12:35-1:00 p.m. ~ Session three (examen)

1:00-1:45 p.m. ~ Personal prayer and reflection time

1:45-2:00 p.m. ~ Closing (large group interaction via chat comments or prayer exercise)

RESOURCES

This content is also on the Sensible Shoes prayer cards. These cards are available as a part of the Sensible Shoes Participant Kit and the Sensible Shoes Leader Kit but are not available separately.

Prayer of Examen

* Quiet yourself in the presence of God. Give God thanks for some of the gifts of today.

* Ask the Holy Spirit to guide and direct your thoughts as you prayerfully review your day.

* When were you aware of God's presence today? When did God seem hidden? In what ways did you respond to God's call? Resist God? How were you brought to life? When were you discouraged?

* Speak honestly with God about whatever you notice. Celebrate the gifts. Confess your sins. Offer your grief. Receive God's grace and comfort.

* In light of what you've noticed about your life with God today, how might you live tomorrow differently?

Labyrinth: A Sacred Journey of Prayer

* The trip inward: Release to God your distractions, burdens, fears. Pray with a Scripture verse or ask God a question for discernment.

* Time at the center: Rest in God's loving presence. Receive whatever gifts of wisdom, peace, or revelation God gives.

* The trip outward: Allow the Spirit to strengthen and empower you as you take God's presence and gifts out into the world.

PRAYERS FOR A GROUP MEETING

Katherine's Prayer Before Spiritual Direction

Jesus Christ, Light of the World, come and light the dark corners of our lives. Where we are blind, grant us sight. Where we stumble in darkness, illumine our path. Quiet us with your love, and enable us to hear your still, small voice. For you are our dear friend, Lord, and we long to be fully present to you.

Prayer for a Group Meeting

Lord, let us hear your voice speaking tenderly to us. Grant us your comfort and your peace. Meet us in the wilderness of our fear, shame, sorrow, or regret. Clear away any obstacles that hinder your coming into our lives, and make straight paths for us to travel more deeply into your heart of love. In Jesus' name. Amen.

Based on Isaiah 40:1-3; adapted from Katherine's prayer, Sensible Shoes, p. 223.

A Blessing

May you grow in the knowledge of God's deep love for you. May you learn to relax into God and rest in his power and faithfulness. May you find opportunities to love God and love others. And since God made us for life together, may you find trustworthy companions to walk with you along the way.

Personalizing Scripture Prayer Exercise

But now thus says the LORD,
 he who created you, O [insert your name];
 he who formed you, O [insert your name]:
Do not fear, for I have redeemed you;
 I have called you by name, you are mine.
When you pass through the waters, I will be with you;
 and through the rivers, they shall not overwhelm you;
when you walk through fire you shall not be burned,
 and the flame shall not consume you.
Based on Isaiah 43:1-2.

ALSO AVAILABLE

The Sensible Shoes

PARTICIPANT'S KIT

BOXED KIT INCLUDES

Sensible Shoes
BOOK

Sensible Shoes
JOURNAL

Sensible Shoes
STUDY GUIDE

Sensible Shoes
PRAYER CARDS
(NOT SHOWN)

The Sensible Shoes Series

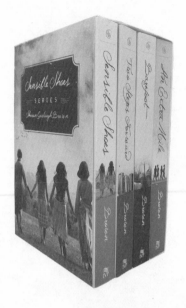

Sensible Shoes
Two Steps Forward
Barefoot
An Extra Mile

STUDY GUIDES

For more information about the Sensible Shoes series,
visit ivpress.com/sensibleshoesseries.
To learn more from Sharon Garlough Brown or to sign up for her newsletter,
go to ivpress.com/sharon-news.